CYNTHIA JAMES

Revealing Your
EXTRAORDINARY
Essence

Practical Tools for Empowered Living

ISBN: 0-9846342-2-3

Art Direction and Cover Design: Launa Fujimoto
lfujimoto@q.com

Photography: Carl Studna
carlstudna.com

Cover Image: Galifax | Dreamstime.com

Editor: Barbara Munson - www.munsoncommunications.com

Please visit the website for more information:
www.cynthiajames.net

A Books to Believe In Publication
Proudly Published in the USA by
Thornton Publishing, Inc.
17011 Lincoln Ave., #408 Parker, CO 80134

The greatest gift Life could have made to you is yourself. You are a spontaneous, self-choosing center in Life, in the great drama of being, the great joy of becoming, the certainty of Eternal expansion. You could not ask for more, and more could not have been given.

~Ernest Holmes

GRATITUDES

I could not have completed this book alone and I want to give thanks to some important people who nurtured this project to completion.

My beloved husband, Carl who always sees the best in me and recognizes my gifts in extraordinary ways.

My beloved mother, Susan, who always reminded me to be a light in this world.

My brother, David, who so lovingly reminds me of my talents.

My children and grandchildren who feed my soul.

Marjorie Helms and Lisa Livingstone who continue to hold the high watch for my unfolding destiny. Lisa, special thanks for being the first pair of eyes to look at the text.

Barbara Munson for her loving spirit and incredible editing expertise.

Rebecca Finkel for working with me to see the vision of the layout into form.

Dr. Roger Teel and the Mile Hi ministerial team and staff. Your belief in me makes my heart smile.

James and Debra Rouse for the enthusiastic "yes" that you bring to my life.

Jean Hendry and Karen Thomas for holding the "high vision" with me.

My prayer partner, Doug, who consistently stands with me as a powerful light and supporter.

EJ Thornton for seeing my potential as an author.

Launa Fujimoto for being patient while co-creating a beautiful cover.

Students, clients and workshop participants, you inspire me with your courage and willingness to grow.

I am eternally grateful for the grace in my life that guides me through the portals of my unfolding destiny.

INTRODUCTION

Let me start by saying that I love being alive. I am excited every day to get up and see what incredible gifts await me. Many people label me as enthusiastic because I am committed to living full out in each moment. I love people seeing me in that way since the etymology of the word enthusiasm actually includes "divine inspiration." I totally feel inspired and motivated to be all that I came here to be. I remember the first time I took a risk, dared to be vulnerable, and it paid off. I felt like I could fly. It was that moment that I began to explore the possibility that feeling this way was my natural state of being. What came forward was an understanding that the core of who I am is magnificent and infinitely EXTRAORDINARY. That discovery set me off on a path that has me committed to supporting others to experience the same revelation. That is exciting to me. It is powerful to witness someone receive the knowledge that he or she is here to serve and make a difference on this planet.

The book is about moving from the ordinary to the EXTRAORDINARY. It is for busy people who want to become more conscious and successful. By busy, I mean that the plate is full with demands and responsibilities that take up an inordinate amount of time. It is for people who feel overwhelmed, overworked and over-committed. It is for people who feel stuck and want to birth "that something" inside of them that is screaming to be released in exceptional ways. The words that come to mind when I think of being EXTRAORDINARY are exceptional, uncommon, unusual, impressive, remarkable and unexpected.

From my point of view, every person on this planet has the ability to express and radiate these qualities. I cannot see any reason that a person would be born to be ordinary, common, unimpressive or uninteresting. How could that be? If each person is filled with potential and infinite possibilities, there must be a delivery system or systems to fully express the gifts encoded in our consciousness. I am aware of the unspoken belief that some people are better than others or have come here to be spectacular beings. I don't agree. The people we place on those pedestals are simply the people who remember that they have an EXTRAORDINARY ESSENCE.

I have been teaching, coaching and facilitating for many years and the one thing that I have gleaned is that people want to be successful. They want to live a life that is filled with joy, love, peace and prosperity. They need tools and they are seeking. They need easy to understand examples that can guide and support them to stay on track.

The self-help market is huge. Billions of dollars are spent annually on books, workshops, seminars and personal coaching. So, why are people still struggling? That is where my mission comes into play. I am committed to support people being in inspired, successful and free. My intention is to provide information that will assist you in moving out of intellectual understanding and into heart-centric experiential success. This book is designed to do that.

Whenever I deliver a talk or facilitate a workshop or webinar, I hear the same question: "How can I keep going so that the old habits don't creep back in and take over my life?" My answer is always the same: YOU MUST PRACTICE. There is no magical formula or fairy godmother who will drop in and instantly shift a life. Every master in the world practices to stay tuned up. It does not matter if it is sports, entertainment, corporate or academia. The people who inspire us the most are proficient in practice.

We live in a culture that places a lot of attention and advertising dollars on acquiring something. That could mean jobs, relationships, money, power or status. It is wonderful to feel comfortable, but, in my mind, it is better to be joyous and fulfilled. That state comes from being connected to self and being clear about how our thoughts and behaviors affect the environments we inhabit. The EXTRAORDINARY person is awake, available and authentic. That means they are conscious in how they live, respond and express. The truth is, no one is ordinary and everyone has the potential of expressing in a state of the EXTRAORDINARY. Join me as together we "bust the myth" that it is normal to be ordinary and leap into the EXTRAORDINARY life that awaits you.

HOW TO USE THIS BOOK

The book was created to be a support mechanism. Therefore, there are chapters and sub-sections in each chapter. Each chapter has a title that explains the area to be explored (e.g., Love, Power, Purpose). The sub-sections have more specific titles to support certain life experiences or challenges. These are followed by exercises that will enhance the topic. Everything is designed to open new perspectives and refocus non-supportive beliefs. The exercises are not long or complicated. This is where the practice comes in. Your mind and old patterns work in tandem to keep you stuck. You will hear the mind chatter about how busy you are and how you don't have time to do all of this stuff. It will try to convince you that the discomfort you are feeling is "bearable" and you can live with it—but is that really how you want to live? That state feels "ordinary" to me. Why not decide to move forward and see if a change in your habits could really change your life? You will be able to measure your growth simply by your commitment to the exercises.

Affirmations and quotes also are included throughout the book to support your experience. I invite you to read the quotes as reminders of what is available for you. The affirmations are short but they have a lot to say. You can write them on cards that you carry with you or just memorize them on an as-needed basis. The more you say positive words like these, the more your mind will move into alignment with easy and empowered living.

In many of the sections there are questions. Asking the right questions engages the mind in looking for answers that move us into positive ways of reacting and responding. We are always asking questions, but many of us are asking from the perspective of the victim. The questions in this book will create new thinking patterns and neuro-pathways that can guide you to more expansive choices.

There is no perfect way to move though the book. You can do it at your own pace and in any way that calls you. However, here are a couple of thoughts.

1. One way is to utilize the contents of this book as a year-long program of conscious living. Start at the very beginning and do the exercises or a portion of the exercises weekly to keep you on track. You can make it a part of your daily practice if you have one OR create one to accommodate this new way of living.

2. Pick one chapter at a time (an area that challenges you) and focus on it. Keep doing those exercises until you feel more grounded and can see clear shifts in your life. The important thing about this suggestion is that once you see results it will encourage you to move forward and try something new.

3. If you will start 5–15 minutes a day for the exercises, you will begin to immediate see minor shifts. Of course, you can move in an accelerated way if you commit to more time.

Using a journal can be helpful. Label it "MY EXTRAORDINARY ESSENCE" Journal. You can do the exercises, write down thoughts and/or revelations. Use it to document wins and shifts. You can also use it to track patterns and see how they currently affect the life you are living.

However you choose to use it, you will be one step closer to allowing your EXTRAORDINARY ESSENCE to emerge and help you explode into greatness.

Let's agree on one thing: YOU ARE WORTH IT! The time and energy you put into you will pay off one hundredfold and the people around you will benefit from the new you that will emerge.

Thank you for connecting with this book. Please know that I see you as EXTRAORDINARY and am thrilled that you will take this opportunity to discover that truth for yourself. The world will be a better place as you reveal your EXTRAORDINARY ESSENCE.

—CYNTHIA JAMES

TESTIMONIALS

"Cynthia James is one of the most powerful and inspiring teachers and role models I know. I've taken several workshops with her over the years and have learned tools and practices that I use frequently. They have helped me shorten considerably the time I spend in negative or unproductive patterns. They have helped me live more authentically, powerfully and creatively. Thank you, Cynthia!"

—Kumar Dandavati, Principal, The Dandavati Group

"Love is a verb, and Cynthia James teaches us its powerful expression in words, thoughts, intention and deeds. Use this wisdom to focus or refocus the loves of your life, your love for yourself and your love for others."

—Betsy Wiersma, Founder, CampExperience™

"Cynthia James is a gifted speaker and teacher who has the ability to transform an audience with her passion, commitment and grace. She delivers heart opening, life-changing wisdom."

—Arielle Ford, author, *The Soulmate Secret*

"Cynthia James' message is here to inspire the soul. She will help you discover life changing truths and guide you with loving care. Believe and you will receive."

—Gary Quinn, bestselling author,
Living In The Spiritual Zone and Life Coach

"Cynthia James recently worked with my partners and me in establishing an optimal way of working together in a new business venture. Her approach was thorough, compassionate, insightful and effective in supporting each team member."

—GG Johnston, President, Downstream Partners, LLC

"For years I have avoided the business world because I could not stand the corporate politics, competition and bureaucracy. After Cynthia James' incredibly positive presentation I felt like I could rise above and was able to release some of my judgments. I'm really enjoying the contributing to my business team now with a better attitude. Thank you Cynthia for reminding me to embrace it all!"

—Greg Montana (Heart Virtue)

"Cynthia brings a stunning combination of gifts, talents and skills—deep spiritual consciousness, a powerful delivery, her compelling story of transformation, insight into the heart and challenges of others and a mission to serve the revelation of wholeness in all."

—Dr. Kathy Hearn, Community Spiritual Leader,
United Centers for Spiritual Living

"Your talk entitled "Ordinary to Extraordinary" moved not only me, but the entire room. In the hour that I listened to you tell your story along with the stories of other amazing human beings I was inspired to refocus my own perspective on the world and the opportunities that exist within the core of every challenge."

—Jena J. Hausmann, Senior Vice President and
Chief Operating Officer, The Children's Hospital, Denver, Colorado

"Within the first minute she had the entire community in the palm of her hands because of the depth of Spirit that she speaks from, the clarity of her message of hope and transformation and her ability to be authentic and personal."

—Rev. Mark Anthony Lord, Chicago Center for Spiritual Living

TABLE OF CONTENTS

FOREWORD

The wisdom of Christian D. Larsen expressed in the statement describes the essence, mission and life of Reverend Cynthia James. Friend, mentor, coach, teacher and spirited cheerleader, Cynthia James' path is one of service and heart. I know that you are ready to live the life that you were born to live and I know that Cynthia's wisdom and love is perfect for you right now.

> This is our purpose: to live the purest, the largest, the fairest, the most useful, the most beautiful and the most spiritual life possible.
> ~CHRISTIAN D. LARSEN

I have had the honor and deep joy of knowing Cynthia for nearly a decade. She is my sister, my mental equivalent and a committed warrior for light and love and truth. I have watched her invite and guide audiences of thousands to move from their heads full of judgment and disillusionment into their hearts with courage and conviction to create transformation in their lives. You are blessed with undeniable belief in your highest possibility and expression when you have the gift of being with Cynthia, knee to knee and soul to soul—this book is that gift and the blessing. You will recognize yourself in every part of Cynthia's path: the deep questioning and the burning desire to be on fire with purpose, coupled with the grit and grace needed to be the person of your dreams—this is the life and teaching of Cynthia. Her heart-full guidance will elevate your belief, your resilience and commitment to living your extraordinary life—now.

Cynthia James lives her message. She is you, she is me and she is all of us who have endured great loss, faced painful challenges and been brought to our knees and tested to our very core. If you are deep in your work, doing all that you believe you can to move through your dark night, know that Cynthia has lived there too and her teaching will light your way through. You may be ready to take your life's mission and purpose to the highest demonstration of success and fulfillment and Cynthia's teaching and unwavering belief will support you in actualizing your "greatness mission!"

To be fully alive is a practice. Being a student of your life is the essence of discipline and the path towards growing more happiness, love, abundance and peace in your life. The teachings and exercises in the book are powerful—choose to give yourself completely to them. Play with them, own them, respect them and allow them to transform your mind and your body and become the person you came here to be. Our mission is clear: to become and express our Divinity right here and now. The world awaits and is ready for our collective consciousness to catch fire and blaze a new world order. This new order of love and the truth is set in motion when we choose to become more alive. Cynthia is fully alive and this book is the spark to ignite the extraordinary in you!

—Dr. James Rouse

START

People become really quite remarkable when they start thinking that they can do things. When they believe in themselves they have the first secret of success.

~Norman Vincent Peale

Taking Inventory

Welcome to a new beginning. I am meeting so many people who are excited about this time in history. Even though some of the world happenings are challenging, people seem to have a sense that something great is occurring. I, too, am excited and feel that this time of life is a representation of my change in consciousness and new choices.

> You don't have to be great to start, but you have to start to be great.
> ~JOE SABAH

Let us start by really opening to the new possibilities that are available. As I was contemplating this, I thought about the fact that stores always do an inventory of product when they are ready to bring in new merchandise. It is at this point that items go on sale to move them out of the store and we, as consumers, look for the deals. All of this made me think about the fact that it might be time for you to do a personal inventory of your current life and choices. It is an incredible process because it includes relationships, work, creativity and finances. You will have the chance to look at how you view your life and what areas need to be cleared out to make room for the new.

EXERCISE:

1. **Make a list of the areas that are important to you.** These could be family, friends, work, money, spirituality, health and self-care.

2. **Choose the three that resonate with you the most.** Write, honestly, about how you are doing in each area. There may be good

news and interesting news for you. Some of the areas may feel strong and clear; other areas may feel cluttered and disconnected.

3. **Choose the areas that "feel" strong and create affirmations about them.** Affirmations are positive statements that sound as if they are already occurring. Stating them often will continue to anchor these feelings.

4. **Choose one challenge in each area and create an intention statement.** Example: *My intention is to be more expressive.* Intentions seed experience.

5. **Commit to read your intentions daily for one month.**

6. **In this moment, that is all you need to do.** Open to a powerful and complete shift in these areas.

Note: By not creating a goal or to-do list, which will limit you, you open yourself to guidance for the expansion and growth in each of these areas beyond what you currently understand or want. Be excited to experience what comes in. I wish for you a magical, mystical and extraordinary revelation!

affirmation: Today, I am open to inner guidance as I examine my amazing life. I am committed to being clearer and stronger. I am powerful and I claim it.

High Vibrational Living

David Hawkins, MD, PhD, an internationally renowned psychiatrist, author and pioneer in the fields of consciousness research and spirituality, has done a lot of research around vibrational energy and its effects on human behavior. He discovered that vibrations of 200 MHz or better are more supportive for conscious living. Basically, he says that if you correlate with this frequency in thought, word, deed and behavior, you begin to create healthy living. There is much discussion on how attitude relates to experience. Consider how focus affects vibration and therefore informs what you will attract into your life.

> Start by doing what's necessary; then do what's possible; and suddenly you are doing the impossible.
> ~ST. FRANCIS OF ASSISI

There was a challenge in my life that pulled most of my attention. I thought about it, talked about it and prayed about it. Then, one day I spoke to an incredible woman in my life who is an energy coach. She shared with me that the approach that I was taking was lowering my vibration and frequency because it was focused on what was wrong. A great "aha" occurred in that moment. By being where I was, I could only become sadder, more tired, and feel more pain. So, I created a statement that I would use whenever my mind would want to take me into that fear and pain place. I simply called in love and light. I know that sounds simple and, at first, I repeated it a lot. Then I realized that I was creating a new habit and thus expanding my vibration and field of positive experience. The shift has been amazing. I now use that energy statement to place my attention on creating a more powerful and enriching life. I also use it to be in higher service to myself, others and community.

I invite you to start discovering your extraordinary essence by observing your thought patterns and how they make you feel. If you do not feel joyous, hopeful, expansive or powerful, you are vibrating at a lower frequency.

EXERCISE: Create your own "energy shift statement." Make it simple and easy to remember. Examples: *I choose love* OR *Peace fills my heart*. Notice that when you say it, you relax, feel more comfortable or simply smile. Use this statement consistently and see what happens.

affirmation: Today, I call in the highest vibrations that life has to offer.

Begin Again, part I

It is not a secret that each new day brings an opportunity to start over. I believe that intention and goal setting are powerful tools. However, saying that you want to change is not enough. Change comes about when there is a willingness to shift patterns and behaviors that do not serve our health and well-being. Statistics show that a majority of people fail to succeed using only resolutions and goals. The reason is simple: people are trying to adjust from the outside. This is often not supportive. Lasting transformation occurs on the inside and is connected to purpose and willingness. In this segment, I will give you some tools to support the creation of deeply rooted intentions that stand the test of time. In Part II, I will support you in ways that will anchor long-term commitments.

> Take the first step in faith. You don't have to see the whole staircase, just take the first step.
> ~MARTIN LUTHER KING JR

EXERCISE:

1. **Write down an intention statement of what you want your life to look like going forward.** Dream BIG. Do not let limited thinking get in the way. How will you be living? What kind of people will be in your life? How will you look? How will you take care of your body? How will you make a difference in the world? How will you relate to money? How will you serve your family, community and friends?

2. **Make a list of the things that ignite you (passion points).** Passion is the number one thing that will keep you motivated, even in challenging times. Successful people are doing things that inspire them. Choose your top three.

3. Make a list of things that do not support you (pain points).
People usually give up because their pain points gradually take over their thinking and behaviors. Choose your top three.

Become aware of how you want to live and then close your eyes and "feel" that vision in your body. It may take a few times but do not give up. Once you "feel" it you can find it again. This will activate within you, an energy of success. Doing it first thing in the morning is powerful and will be a great start to the day. I encourage you to work on this every day. We will work with the passion and pain points in Part II.

It is important that you affirm success. Your old ways of operating have been there a long time and want to stay alive. When past behaviors surface, it is a sign that you are moving beyond your pain into your passion. Stay strong. I believe in you. You are a masterpiece in the making and have come here to do great things.

affirmation: Today, I claim my power and purpose. I am destined to do great things and I am unstoppable.

Begin Again, part II

In the first segment of Begin Again, you started practicing "feeling" success. If you have not been able to do it everyday, do not "beat yourself up." Everything is a process and it may take some work. Activating willingness is a key. The intention statement is the visualization of the life that you want to live. Being willing to live a vibrant and vital life will propel you into success.

> Do not wait until the conditions are perfect to begin. Beginning makes the conditions perfect.
> ~ALAN COHEN

You also identified your passion and pain points. The passion points are the things that bring joy into your heart and make you feel alive. When you learn to lead with passion you cannot help but be excited about fully participating in life. People who live with passion have an infectious way of being. We want to be around them. Passionate people make us smile.

Pain points are the areas that keep us from succeeding. They are strong critical voices that continue to tell you of your flaws and character defects. The pain points are distractions that keep you from living full out. They are well-practiced in talking you out of being successful. Once you become familiar with their energy, you will see how they affect your body, your thinking and your choices. It is very empowering when we realize that we are at choice in igniting our passion while releasing non-supportive beliefs.

EXERCISE:

In the next two weeks, I invite you to do the following:

1. **Write one affirmation for each of your top three passion points.** Example: *I am joyously expressing my creativity in inspiring ways every day, OR I am enthusiastically shining my light everywhere I am.* These affirmations will become anchors in supporting the realization of your intention.

2. **Write one statement that shifts each of your top three pain points into power.** Example: *I joyously care for my body by eating in a healthy way and exercising my body, OR I am choosing to release negative thinking and open to the possibilities of my life everyday.* These statements will be expansive as you divorce the inner critic voice and step into your personal power.

Get a 3x5 card and write your affirmation on one side and your shift statement on the other. Carry it with you and read them aloud. Some days you will only need to read them once. Other days you may need to read them multiple times. Here is the key: You must commit to this wholeheartedly. Do this for 30 days and you will instill a new habit that is supportive and energizing.

Continue bringing forward this "feeling" of success daily. This will keep the vision of your new and improved life fully activated. If you think about practicing a sport, for example, it might make it easier. You do not become good at tennis or golf unless you practice often.

There is nothing and no one that can stop you but you. Keep your eye on the prize. There is a winner in you.

affirmation: Today, I stand on the precipice of my greatness and I dare to soar.

LOVE

A loving heart is the beginning of all knowledge.

~Thomas Carlyle

THE POWER OF LOVE

This day focuses on the power of love. There is not a person on the planet who does not respond to love. Love is healing and transformative. Love is nurturing and comforting. Love is an energy that opens the heart and supports deepening in relationships.

> Blessed is the influence of one true, loving human soul on another.
> ~GEORGE ELIOT

I would like to invite you to explore how love expresses in your life, beginning with love of self. I was once at a conference in which spiritual teacher Iyanla Vanzant gave this amazing presentation about her new love. She had everyone spellbound for several minutes and then she announced that her new love was herself. She had discovered that she was the one she had been waiting for.

Do you know that about yourself? Are you clear about what makes you happy, what kind of life you deserve? Do you treat yourself as if you are the beloved you have been waiting for? Do you honor yourself and treat yourself with respect?

A teacher once told me that I would never experience deep loving with a partner if I could not learn to love and appreciate myself. Nothing could have been more revelatory. My husband appeared in my life when I realized the importance of loving me.

EXERCISE:

Take some time to really explore how you love yourself.

- Write down the ways you honor yourself.
- Write down the ways you do not honor yourself.
- Choose which one will be your way of operating this week.

I hope that you will choose to honor yourself in every way imaginable. You are loveable and worthy of deep and abiding love.

affirmation: Today, I actively begin to focus on loving and appreciating the beautiful person that I am.

THE POWER OF LOVE

The definition of lavish is to give in great amounts. Let us just say that today is Valentine's Day and what an interesting day it is. For some, it represents a great day for gift giving, mostly with flowers and candy. For others, it is just a reminder that they are without a partner to share this time with. I remember a time when I would buy myself flowers to remind me that I was loved. Then, during this time, I began to realize that I could create loving acts for others and become a space of service. It made a huge difference in my life and the life of others.

> Being deeply loved by someone gives you strength, while loving someone deeply gives you courage.
> ~LAO TZU

Many of the greatest teachers tell us that the simple act of giving opens the heart and creates a field of connection and devotion. This giving creates a "love boomerang" effect. We give without being desirous of anything and surprisingly we are given more than we could possibly imagine.

EXERCISE:

Make this week Valentine's week in your heart and lavish love on everyone you meet. Give great amounts of love, appreciation and acknowledgment to everyone you encounter. Treat everyone as if they are precious and deserving of your full attention.

If you do this, I guarantee you that lavish love will be returned to you a hundredfold. People will mirror back your kindness and consideration in ways that you cannot imagine.

REMEMBER:

- You are a gift in my life and to this planet.
- You are an amazing soul who has a great destiny.
- Your willingness to grow warms my heart.
- Your presence makes a difference wherever you are.

affirmation: Today, I make it my personal mission to bring joy into someone's life.

The Energy of Love

The energy of love is powerful and transcendent. It can break down the walls of resentment and disappointment and move people to places of acceptance and healing. The energy of love can alter the ways in which people move through the most challenging of times. Love can shift any relationship because it can be felt in the heart beyond any words that can be said.

> Love is like energy. It can never be created nor destroyed.
> ~IAN PHILPOT

I have counseled many people who are challenged in relationships or moving through painful divorces. Without fail, people find it hard to move away from judgments or expressions of anger and fear. Because I have had my own challenges in this area, I could share with them what I have learned. When I was moving through a challenging divorce, I was feeling sad and disillusioned. I was leaving a restaurant and a thought softly entered my mind. The message, "Love is an eternal energy, form changes but love remains," seemed to wash over me. It was one of those "aha" moments in which you recognize that you have been gifted with an amazing truth. That was the moment that my healing began. I made a choice to give thanks for my marriage and dedicate my energy to creating a new life.

EXERCISE:
- Get a picture of someone who challenges you and put it on an altar or somewhere you can see it daily.

- Send that person love daily using a phrase similar to "I wish for you the same love I wish for myself."
- There might be a part of you that resists, but do it anyway. The person's soul can receive the love even if the actual person cannot in this moment.
- There will come a time that you will see and/or experience a complete shift in the way you think about or relate to this person.

This exercise is for you! The more love you send out, the more it comes back to you!

affirmation: I use my energy to create a life that radiates harmony.

INFUSING LOVE INTO LIFE

Most of the people in my life love to eat. Food is the topic of many conversations and finding great food is a quest of many of my friends and loved ones. I have often been amazed at how people become ecstatic when they taste extraordinary food. I believe it is because when food is cooked with love and passion it enhances the taste and energetically connects with the people eating the food. Let me give you an example. I recently attended a party held by a hostess who loved to bake. When I arrived, she was making chocolate cupcakes with caramel icing. I have had many cupcakes but nothing that tasted like this. I watched her back as she lovingly put the icing on the cupcakes, and I could feel the love that she was placing into that cake.

> Love cannot endure indifference. It needs to be wanted. Like a lamp, it needs to be fed out of the oil of another's heart, or its flame burns low.
> ~HENRY WARD BEECHER

What if we infused that kind of love into every aspect of our lives? What if we were so passionate that we placed love in our interactions, our emails, our projects and presentations? What if we did that without anyone knowing and then just sat back and witnessed the reactions? I believe that we would begin to experience responses that would be amazing.

EXERCISE:
- Choose an area where you want to experiment with this concept: cooking, writing, singing, shopping for a gift, your hobby, creating art, cleaning your home, etc.

- Anything that you do in this area, add loving thoughts and energy before you complete it or share it.
- Document or journal the responses you get.

Have fun. I guarantee you that love infused into the things you do will transform the way you experience your life.

affirmation: Today, I become a master chef of life. I place love into every activity.

CONNECT

I always think it's
interesting to dig a little
bit deeper every time
you go to someplace that
seems like a revelation
or a strong connection to
an emotional truth.

~Carly Simon

Oneness

There is a lot of talk about oneness and unity today. Many teachers are telling us that we are all connected and interconnected. The recent movie, Avatar, shows an entire culture that is practicing oneness with each other and with nature. So why is it so difficult for us to actually live in that place? Why is it so difficult to actually live with a deep understanding that everything we do, say and think affects the Whole?

> If we have no peace, it is because we have forgotten that we belong to each other.
> ~MOTHER TERESA

You are not alone. In fact, your energy, your essence and your way of being have an impact on everything around you.

Think about entering a room where you instantly feel an energy that makes you uncomfortable. Where does that energy come from? How about when you meet someone for the first time and your instinct is to withdraw? Take this one step further. You are challenged with a colleague or a client. Whenever you see or are about to meet this person, your body becomes tense and constricted. You try to calm yourself, pray or even create affirmations—to no avail. You resolve to not let him or her bother you, but most of the time that tactic does not work.

Do you think that the other person can feel your discomfort? Absolutely! He or she feels it and reacts to it! People also respond to peaceful and authentic energy. Have you ever walked into a space and witnessed someone who is light and charismatic? The person is vibrating at such a high level that you cannot help but be drawn to him or her. In fact, if you are really paying attention, you will see that many people are drawn to this person. Energy and the expression of it have an effect on life.

What kind of person do you want to be? How do you want to affect your family, community or work environment? You can choose right this very minute.

EXERCISE:
- Picture the person who challenges you and imagine him or her as a child wanting to be loved and seen.
- Affirm that you and this other person are here to support one another's growth.
- Declare:"I see the budding genius in you and support your freedom."

If you do this every day for several weeks, something will change. **You will!** Your need to be distant and judgmental will decrease and you will begin to feel and sense the oneness present with you and this other person. Peace will unfold, or the other person will be moved to another place that supports his or her greatness.

I have had clients report back to me that using this tool has completely changed their relationships and opened up new avenues for peace and abundance.

affirmation: Today, I place my full attention on the energy I bring. I commit to bringing the best of who I am into every moment.

THE ART OF BEING PRESENT

Have you ever been with someone and you are sharing from a place of vulnerability and he or she seems distracted? How do you feel? What decision do you make about the person you are with? You decide that he is not present and you probably begin to shut down on some level. I would venture to say that some judgment comes in that creates separation between you and this other person.

> Don't let yesterday use up too much of today.
> ~CHEROKEE INDIAN PROVERB

Let's talk about you. How are you at being present with others? Do you find yourself thinking about what you need to do next, the deadlines that are coming up or who you just saw walk in the door? Guess what? You have now done to someone else what made you feel uncomfortable and unheard. You have just created the beginning of a breakdown that is non-supportive for you and the other person.

The art of being present requires that you are completely with another person. Your intention is to see them and hear what they are saying. Your intention is to give them your attention so fully that they feel safe. For some people, it will be the first time they have had this experience. In 1999, I had the opportunity to be around the Dalai Lama for several days. This man has completely mastered the art of being present with others and with himself. He listens intently and responds from a place of complete authenticity. This way of being was so inspiring that I made a commitment to practice being present. It is not always easy, but when I master it people genuinely give thanks from a deep place of heart.

EXERCISE:

- Breathe in slowly the intention to be present.
- Activate a willingness to be completely in the moment with the other person.
- Open your heart so you can "feel" the connection.
- Mirror back what the other person has said when appropriate.
- Gently come back to the breath if you feel your mind wandering.
- Thank the person for being with you and let him or her know how much you have appreciated the sharing.
- Take a moment to honor yourself for practicing the art of being present.

affirmation: Today, I give to others what I want to receive. I consciously create a safe space by being present and honoring each person I meet.

HEART CENTERED LISTENING

I am very grateful to have completed a course in Spiritual Psychology from the University of Santa Monica. One of the first skills we learned was called "heart centered" listening. This tool is defined as consciously entering the heart and listening from a deep place of compassion and caring. We learned that to listen from the heart demonstrates respect. It shows interest in the person in front of you, creates a safe space and communicates an attitude of willingness to be present and open.

> Heart-centered people listening to their heart's voice do affect others energetically. The heart-focused people can in fact collectively affect the world community on a large scale.
> ~GREGG BRADEN

Just think about this! What would you feel like if someone was with you in this way? The first time I experienced heart centered listening all of my protective devices dropped. It reminded me that when someone listens to me in this way it is easy to open up and share. It is easy to relax and let go. I believe that everyone wants to feel this way when they are with another person. We all want to experience someone being so committed to hearing us that joy fills every fiber of our being.

As I utilized this tool with clients something amazing happened. People opened up and moved quickly into a space of vulnerability. Business acquaintances told me that they felt comfortable working together. In fact, clients referred me to others with the recommendation that I was a caring and committed person.

I invite you to begin to practice heart centered listening. You can start with a family member or a friend. Or, if you feel brave, you can begin with colleagues at work. Wherever you choose to start be aware that it takes practice. No one is masterful from the beginning. Do not be hard on yourself if it takes a while to become proficient.

EXERCISE:
- Set an intention to listen from the heart and to be connected.
- Connect to your heart physically and mentally, and call in "loving." (Loving energy is healing.)
- Let the person know that you are with him or her and interested in what the person has to say.
- Simply listen from the heart.

I believe you will find that other people feel connected to you and you also feel a bond with them. It will make communication easier and more fluid.

affirmation: Today, I commit to listening with my heart.

THE NAMASTE PRINCIPLE

The meaning of the word namaste in Sanskrit, *namah +
te = namaste,* is "I bow to you." The reason why we
practice namaste has a deeper significance. It recognizes the
belief that the life force, the divinity, the Self or the light in
me is the same in all. In some tradi-
tions, bringing the palms together is a
way of honoring another. Some just
say or think the word when someone
enters their space. Either way, it is
acknowledging this kind of oneness
that allows us to behold the beautiful
essence in every person we meet. What
an incredible world we would live in if we saw each other
this way. We would instantly recognize that the universe is rep-
resented in each individual soul. We could move through each
day, bowing in complete acknowledgment, internally or ex-
ternally, that we are all gifts and here to do great work.

> Don't believe what your
> eyes are telling you. All they
> show is limitation. Look with
> your understanding, find out
> what you already know, and
> you'll see the way to fly.
> ~**RICHARD BACH**

How are you doing in this area? I know it is easy to recognize
those close to us, but what about the people we experience
as living so completely differently that it challenges us? They
may even cause us to constrict and become judgmental. In
those cases, activating the namaste principle becomes more
difficult. It bumps up against our resistance and our deepest
fears. It anchors in us a feeling of separation and does not
allow a willingness to understand one another.

We are here to make a difference in this world and it begins when we accept that everyone is important and on a path of growth and discovery. There is no one on this planet who does not want to love and be loved. There is no one who does not want to be healthy and to create safety for their families. There is no one who does not want to feel important and powerful.

EXERCISE:

- Create an intention to be the change you want to see in the world.
- Activate the namaste principle each morning when you awake. Decide to see the light in each person you meet or interact with.

You are an amazing gift to this world and you will feel this from the inside out as you practice and lead your life with namaste.

affirmation: Today, I salute the true essence of every individual. I see them as whole.

CLEAR

As you become more clear about who you really are, you'll be better able to decide what is best for you—the first time around.

~Oprah Winfrey

Spring Clearing

I use the word clearing instead of cleaning because I feel strongly that clearing something out is about releasing— it does not return. With cleaning, you do it over and over again. Do you know people who spring clean every year and to them it is a huge task? Then, the next year they do it all over again. Perhaps that is you!

> Do the thing you fear to do and keep on doing it...that is the quickest and surest way ever yet discovered to conquer fear.
> ~DALE CARNEGIE

I have been looking at the patterns from my family and how it has always been easy to accumulate. I discovered that we did this not because stuff was needed, but because it was about making sure that we had enough. Subtext, there is never enough.

My clients say that clearing out closets has "always been a challenge." I also hear "When I lose weight I am going to wear that again," or "I really like this and I am sure it will come back in style." In reality, they have not lost weight in five years, nor have they worn the outfit for twelve years. These kinds of statements are really about attachment. Buddhists tell us that attachment creates suffering. I add that attachment does not leave room for anything new. It clogs up the flow in our lives.

Where are you in your life? Is it time to look at clearing out anything that does not support the vision you have for your life? Is it time to really look at what you have been holding on to? Take an inventory of your clothes, papers and even relationships. This last one may have caught you by surprise; are you holding on to any relationships that do not nurture or support you? Whatever it is, maybe it is time to take stock of your life.

EXERCISE:

1. Make a list of the areas in your life (home, work, relationships, etc.).
2. Now write in each area the things that could use some clearing.

affirmation: Today, I am dedicating myself to clearing my energy field. I am ready to receive.

CLEARING FROM THE INSIDE-OUT

Everything starts from an intention and then you open to that intention as it is anchored internally. Clearing out in your life must start from deep intentionality. Have you thought about what your life would be like without all the stuff? Have you thought about how you would feel less encumbered?

> Most of us serve our ideals by fits and starts. The person who makes a success of living is the one who sees his goal steadily and aims for it unswervingly. That is dedication.
>
> ~CECIL B. DE MILLE

Think about how you feel when you walk into a clean or clear space. Don't you feel open? That is because the energy is clear. Clear energy opens the heart and activates creativity. People spend a lot of time talking about the life they want to create but then stop when it comes to actualizing this desire.

EXERCISE: Look at the ways you stop your growth. Do not judge, just gently look at them and in your spiritual practice time ask the following questions and also journal.

1. Who am I called here to be?
2. What must I release to be who I came here to be?
3. What will I feel like when I am fully expressing? Really bask in how great it feels to be clear.
4. Look at your world. Does it fit? Do you feel the way you want to feel?

5. If not, it is time to look closely and deeply at what is needing to be released in order to clear and be available for your good.

6. Set an intention for creating clear space in your life. Sit with it and activate a willingness to begin clearing.

It is time for the outside to match the inside.

affirmation: Today, I activate a willingness to be a clear channel for creativity to express as my life.

DARING TO DECLUTTER

The first exercise in this chapter required that you make a list of areas in your life that need clearing. Take out that list and circle one thing in each area. For instance, clean hall closet, let go of old papers I no longer need, have an honest conversation with someone who I feel is consistently disrespectful. If you did not make a list, start one now. I guarantee you that if you do this process you will clear up energy and open the floodgates of flow.

> Three Rules of Work:
> Out of clutter find simplicity;
> From discord find harmony;
> In the middle of difficulty
> lies opportunity.
> ~ALBERT EINSTEIN

Now read closely: Your mind and place of comfort will start talking to you. It may say, "You don't have time to do this now" or "This task is so overwhelming." Your mind is trying to keep you hooked. All you have to do is become daring and willing, taking one step at a time.

EXERCISE:

1. Start with a vision.
2. Pick one thing to work on for 30 days.
3. Continue to visualize how you will feel when this is complete. Do a little at a time.
4. Reward yourself when you complete an area: go to a movie, to a spa or enjoy a meal in a nice restaurant.

Whatever you do is something. Every great person starts with vision and then moves forward; each step brings you closer to your goal. Dare to declutter and open to infinite possibilities.

affirmation: Today, I simplify my life and joyously step into a state of clarity beyond my wildest dreams.

Organizing as a Practice

I know for some of you the word organizing sends shivers up your spine. It does not call to you. However, let me share this with you: it does no good to clear things out if you do not have a system to keep things clear. You will re-create the same old pattern with new stuff.

Julie Morgenstern is a wonderful author who wrote a book called *Organizing from the Inside Out.* Julie has a lot of great information; I am sharing with you a few tips from her book.

> Love life, engage in it, give it all you've got, love it with a passion, because life truly does give back, many times over, what you put into it.
> ~MAYA ANGELOU

One of the things Julie says is to look at what is working and what is not working. From my perspective she is also asking us to look at priorities. What do you need to be successful and what is in the way?

EXERCISE: Five easy steps from *Organizing from the Inside Out*
1. **Sort** – Identify what is important to you (what you currently use and love).
2. **Purge** – You get to decide how: toss it, give it away, recycle or find another way.
3. **Assign a New Home**– Carefully decide where what is left is going to live (such as a drawer, shelf or closet). Be clear!
4. **Containerize** – Containers make it easy to group things and help to limit how much you accumulate. Some people make a container list.
5. **Equalize** – A couple of weeks after you get organized set time

aside to assess where you are and how your system is working. Decide what you need to stay on track. This might be the perfect time to have your accountability partner, if you have one, support you.

I give you my complete support as you are cleared out of anything non-supportive. I see you as completely successful and expansive.

affirmation: Today, I put into practice what I know will support my health and well-being. I call in order in every area of my life.

TRUST

Trust your instinct to the end, though you can render no reason.

~Ralph Waldo Emerson

Awakening Trust

Trust is something that many of us struggle with mostly because we have been disappointed in some way. Let us begin with the definition of trust: confidence in the integrity of a person or thing; reliance on an intention; depending on someone or something.

> He who does not trust enough, will not be trusted.
> ~LAO TZU

Once trust is broken, it is difficult to regain because you move into a state of hyper-vigilance. You start looking for the places you cannot trust. To awaken trust means to become alert and focused on believing in the integrity of ourselves or others.

Oftentimes when I counsel people or have them share in a class, they admit that trusting is one of the hardest areas for them. I believe it is because they do not trust themselves. They do not feel that they are capable of making good decisions or honoring themselves. They have created evidence that they are not clear thinkers or that their "discernment button" got disconnected. The truth is that they have fallen asleep and covered up the ability to listen to inner guidance.

I do not know where you are in your life, but I am asking you to take an honest look at "trust." Are you on guard when you meet people, wanting them to prove themselves? Do you wait for the shoe to drop and for people to show you their "true colors?" Do you feel that you have to protect yourself from people so that you do not get hurt? If the answer to any of these questions is yes, it is time to awaken trust in you.

EXERCISE:

- Journal on trust and how it challenges you in your life. Do not judge anything you write. We are here to become transparent and grow. Just write. Stream-of-consciousness writing (writing without editing) is very powerful and often circumvents mind chatter. It is important to be honest and activate a willingness to shift. Once this writing is complete, you can move into gratitude for the wonderful opportunities to awaken trust that are available.

affirmation: Today, I am committed to being fully awake. I trust that I am supported in every area of my life.

Releasing Betrayal

I do not believe that there is one of us who has not felt left, dishonored, disrespected or cheated. In those moments, there is often disbelief, confusion, anger or outrage. We cannot believe that we are the object of such disloyal acts. Oftentimes, these events happen without warning or explanation. We are left with empty feelings of doubt and fear.

> You leave old habits behind by starting out with the thought: I release the need for this in my life.
> ~WAYNE DYER

It is in these moments that internal decisions get made: you must not have been enough or you would not have been treated that way; you did not do something right or they would not have left; it had to be your fault, you probably should not have been so honest. Whatever the thought is, you somehow look for the blame in yourself until the anger sets in. Then you blame them, the one who betrayed you.

As long as you are in a state of blame, you are holding on to that person. In fact, you are chained to them. Isn't that an interesting thought? Here is the visual. See yourself dragging the person that hurt you everywhere you go. Not so wonderful, is it? There is good news and interesting news. The interesting news is that you will never be free of them as long as you hold on to anger and resentment. The good news is that once you let them go, you create space for your heart's desire.

The truth is that they have been your teachers. They have brought you the gift of gaining clarity about what you do and do not deserve.

EXERCISE:

1. Write down the gifts (growth, self-love, honesty with self) you have been given in each of these relationships. It does not have to be a long list.

2. Then write a thank you note to each person for showing you what you deserve. Place it on an altar or safe place in your home and (now, here is the interesting part) bless each person daily and call in their happiness. You may want to resist, but this simple act will release them once and for all.

affirmation: Today, I consciously let go of any belief that someone else can take away my joy.

Renewing Intuition

Intuition is about "knowing" without a rational explanation. We all have it. It is installed in our DNA. We are connected. What stops us from remembering are life events and circumstances. Experiences occur that shake us to the core and we somehow think it is because we are not connected. We start second guessing ourselves and make up a story that we are confused. I want to remind you that you are never confused. The reality is that you have moved into a state of "trying to figure things out" instead of tapping into your intuitive knowing.

> You have to leave the city of your comfort and go into the wilderness of your intuition. What you'll discover will be wonderful. What you'll discover is yourself.
> ~ALAN ALDA

I will demonstrate. Think of a time when someone was in your life and that person wanted you to do something that did not make you feel comfortable. You wanted to say no but you did not want to hurt the person's feelings. You pondered it but it still did not feel good to do it. You said yes, meaning you denied your intuitive hit. It turned out badly and you were upset. Now, let us go back to the beginning. Your first thought was NO. Then, you started wanting to take care of the other person. That NEVER works. When you start going against what you know to be true, you set yourself up for pain and struggle.

EXERCISE:

- Whenever someone asks you to do something and you feel uncomfortable, say, "Can I think about that and get back to you?"
- If the person does not want to wait, let her know that you cannot commit to that right now. If she is willing to wait, take some time and meditate on it, pray on it and ask, "Will this serve me?" If the answer is no or you continue to feel uncomfortable, do not do it.
- Practice this with large and small things. It takes practice to become in tune with your intuition, but once you do there will be a flow in your life that will be undeniable.

affirmation: Today, I activate my intuition and deeply listen to my inner guidance.

Reconnecting to the Heart

This chapter is about awakening trust. For those of you who are working through this section, you may be having a challenging time. It is not easy to look at places that bring up such discomfort. So, first of all, give yourself credit for being willing to take this journey. I am here to tell you that this work will transform your life. This work is about the heart and opening to joy.

> I've learned that whenever I decide something with an open heart, I usually make the right decision.
> ~MAYA ANGELOU

When you are in a state of non-trust, the heart closes. Think about it. The area around the heart feels constricted. You are not even clear where the pain originates. You only know that the heart feels numb and disconnected. Not only that, but you feel fatigued and distracted. When the heart is closed, you have to work extra hard to be present. You feel scattered and off balance. Most importantly, you feel separate from your true essence. This is a lonely place to be. Sometimes you cannot even describe how you feel in words.

What has happened is that you have stopped trusting yourself and have shut down the one place that can help support your freedom. When you are connected to the heart, it will communicate with you and guide your decisions. I remember having a job offer and not knowing what to do. The man hiring me sensed my confusion and very wisely said, "Ask your heart." The moment I did that I could tell that it was open. I took that job and it turned out to be one of the greatest gifts of my life.

EXERCISE:

- When you need to make a decision, "ask your heart;" if it is open, say yes.
- If the heart is constricted, wait. Do not move. You are being guided to be still.
- This simple act will support you reconnecting and trusting yourself.

affirmation: Today, I honor the intelligence of my heart. I can trust it.

INVEST

Take time to gather up the past so that you will be able to draw from your experiences and invest them in the future.

~Jim Rohn

Eye on the Prize

I am committed to supporting you in living a fulfilled and powerful life and am in awe of your willingness to commit to this process. The focus for this chapter is how you invest in your life and how you discover the dividends that you are receiving.

> It's how you handle adversity, not how it affects you. The main thing is never quit, never quit, never quit.
> ~BILL CLINTON

There has never been a winner in any arena who has not been completely focused on what he or she wants. Every act and decision is connected to achieving their goal. Olympic athletes always hold my great admiration. They do enormous work before the Games and then they compete with immense intentionality. No matter what happens, they "keep their eye on the prize." Remember when diver Greg Louganis hit his head on the diving board and still came back to win the gold? That happened because the challenge was not his focus. He moved into an internal space of focus and allowed himself to envision the perfect dive.

The gold, bronze and silver winners are no different than you; they just know how to keep their eye on the prize.

EXERCISE:

- Did you set an intention for the year? If not, create one; it is never too late.
- If yes, re-visit the intention. Is it strong enough? Is it clear enough? If not, re-state it!

- Pick one word that exemplifies that intention (e.g., powerful, wealthy, freedom).
- Whenever anything happens that starts to pull you off target, say your word as a symbol of keeping you focused.

Invest in you! Stay focused!

affirmation: Today, I invest my whole being into my life. I am focused, clear and unstoppable.

RELATIONSHIP ENDOWMENTS

I n order to bequest or leave an inheritance, there must be
something to leave or give. Many of us are looking for
the "perfect" relationship, but I think we really do not look
at what it takes to have one. I was recently at a dinner and a
beautiful woman shared that she
was looking for her perfect man.
The consensus from the guests in
the conversation was that she would
never find him—he does not exist.

> In every relationship,
> in every moment, we teach
> either love or fear.
> ~**MARIANNE WILLIAMSON**

In fact, what she had in her mind was too fantasy-filled. I do
not know if that is true or not, but the thought did come to
mind. As I looked and listened, I wondered if she had any
idea that she might be looking for the "knight in shining
armor."

To have a meaningful relationship, you must invest in being
the kind of person who creates it. You must create a "relationship endowment" that will leave a lasting experience with
everyone you meet and interact with. You must become the
gift that you are seeking.

I was working with a counselor many years ago and was com-
plaining about my own challenges in relationships. The
counselor drew a picture of six circles surrounding
one circle and then he drew a circle off to the side. He
explained that I was the circle surrounded by the six and that
I wanted them to complete me. The circle off to the side rep-
resented my soul mate. That person was waiting for me to

love myself and become the person he desired as a mate. That was a powerful lesson for me. Where are you? What kind of relationship endowment are you currently creating?

EXERCISE: In your journal, reflect on the following questions from a place of authentic inquiry.

- Do you wait to see what others will do before you show up fully?
- Do you meet people with the expectation that they will be wonderful?
- Do you believe, in your heart of hearts, that you must become what you seek?

In answering these questions, be truthful with yourself. It is important that you begin to look at the energy and beliefs that you currently invest in. If you want to receive love, compassion and heart-centered relating, you must become those things and share them with everyone you meet.

affirmation: Today, I open to becoming the love that I have been seeking. I radiate authentic love in every moment.

THE POWER OF LOVE

Contemplate this statement: pre-approved, sign up now! Most of us are familiar with this sales tool. We get mail all of the time from credit card companies telling us that they have the best deal for us and we are pre-approved. That means we are important, valuable and trust-worthy. Or does it? Of course, we all know this is a marketing ploy. But, I believe that statement is actually a universal statement of our unique expression.

> Without an understanding of who we are, and from where we came, I do not think we can truly advance.
> ~LOUIS B. LEAKEY

When you think about it, you came here with a stamp of approval. You came here as a complete package of beauty, power, light and creativity. The universe said, YES! This person is exactly what we need to fulfill this perfect destiny. Your worth and full expression have nothing to do with putting your name on a document to get a credit card or purchasing a piece of merchandise. You sign up when you say YES to life!

Some of you may be thinking: we all say yes to life. I would beg to differ here. Some people absolutely say NO to anything that will make them more visible and powerful. Here is how:

- They refuse to take care of themselves.
- They spend a majority of their time in negative reaction or relationships.
- They do only what will "get them by."

Any of these things and tons more that we can think of tell the Universe that we are not ready to live a big life.

EXERCISE: Write down all the ways you currently do not sign up for an amazing life. Journal on these questions:
- Do you refuse to take care of yourself?
- Do you spend a majority of your time in negative reaction?
- Do you stay in negative relationships even though you know you should leave?
- Do you refuse opportunities to show up in more powerful ways?
- Do you do only what will "get you by?"

affirmation: Today, I sign up for life! I am ready, open and available and I say YES!

Continuous Deposits

Any of you who are saving some of your income are clear that you have to continuously deposit money into your bank account if you wish it to grow. In order to save, you must be committed to building up that account and to resisting withdrawing any amount. Here is where it gets tricky. A lot of us think we are committed until some big need arises and then we deplete the account with the commitment that we will return the money as soon as we can. Oftentimes we never do because life takes over. Then, we sit in a quandary about why we are so challenged financially.

> Even the thought of giving, the thought of blessing, or a simple prayer has the power to affect others.
> ~DEEPAK CHOPRA

This is what I would like you to consider. What are you depositing into your life account? Are you putting in health, passionate living, joyous relationships and clear financial choices? Are you making these deposits when it feels good and, then, when life gets challenging you choose to put your attention and energy elsewhere with the promise that you will get back to this good stuff when you can? There is no better time than now. There is nothing more important than you and the fullness of life that calls you. Where you put your attention grows. What you place as a seed in the universe grows.

Please consider that you are an essential part of the universal scheme. Quantum science tells us that we are all connected.

If that is true, you are here to be your best to make a difference on this planet. You are here to share your best self. Every time that you show up fully you enhance all life.

EXERCISE:

- Please look at where you continuously deposit your time and energy.
- Look at where you feel depleted and see how often you have withdrawn your love or life energy.
- Make a commitment to continuously deposit only things that support your health and well being.

affirmation: Today, I place into the world what I want to receive. I make a difference because I exist.

SING

A bird doesn't sing because it has an answer, it sings because it has a song.

~Maya Angelou

WINNER IN YOU

I love music! As long as I have been a singer, I have used music to heal and transcend challenges. In fact, often times I choose songs because of the messages that inspire me. In this chapter, we will look at four songs that I hope will ignite something in you. They would not be called "spiritual songs," but they do have a message for the spirit. The first song is "Winner in You." This song was composed by songwriters Ashford and Simpson for a Broadway show starring Patti LaBelle. The show did not do well, but this song stood out. The words to the chorus are what I want to share with you today.

> You can't be a winner
> and be afraid to lose.
> ~**CHARLES LYNCH**

There's a winner
There's a hero
There's a lover too
Somewhere there's a winner in you.

Wouldn't it be incredible if you remembered this song, these lyrics whenever "stuff" was happening in your life that seemed "off?" There IS a winner in you. There is something in you that is unstoppable and unbeatable. There is something in you that is the stuff heroes are made of. There is something in you that is loveable and loving, joyous and expansive. Wow! If you knew that, you would look at every situation as an opportunity to show your winner self to the world. You would walk with confidence, dare to risk, speak with authority and step out into the world each day knowing that you are destined to win.

EXERCISE:

Why not act as if?

- Declare yourself a winner before you leave your house each day.
- Walk with energy and confidence.
- Say yes to something new, even if you do not know how to do it.
- Share your thoughts in areas where you are usually quiet.

affirmation: Today, I claim and proclaim that I am a winner in every area of my life.

Never Been to Me

Nancy Wilson is one of my all-time favorite singers. She sang a song, among others, called "Never Been to Me." The moment I heard it, I knew I had to sing it. There was never a time that I sang that song that it did not affect people. It is a song about a woman who had these life experiences that seemed grand and sometimes awful and through it all she had never met herself. I so resonated with that song because it was as if someone had seen my life and written a song about it. Here is the part of the song that I want to share:

> There is no finer sensation in life than that which comes with victory over one's self. Go forward to a goal of inward achievement, brushing aside all your old internal enemies as you advance.
> ~VASH YOUNG

I've no doubt you dream about the things you'll never do
but I wish someone had a talked to me
like I wanna talk to you…
I've been to paradise, but I've never been to me.

It is so interesting to me that so many of us are in "search mode." We are looking for ourselves everywhere that we are not. There is some misconception that we are going to find our happiness in more money, the right relationship, the perfect job or house. We are going to be comfortable as soon as our parents understand and honor us. None of these things has anything to do with peace. You are the thing you have been looking for and if you stop long enough you will discover that within you are the answers to all of the questions.

EXERCISE:

1. Think about all the "things" and "stuff" that you believe will make your life better. Write them down.

2. Think about all the good things that are in your life right now (e.g., you are alive, your children are healthy, you have a car, you have a home). Write them down.

3. Look at the first list. Is there anything on that list that will bring you long-lasting peace? No, there is not. These "things" might bring you comfort, but the peace you seek lives within your spirit.

What if you knew that your life was complete in every moment just because you exist? The answer to this question is something for you to contemplate.

affirmation: Today, I celebrate the original, magnificent me.

STAND

Some of you are old enough to remember Sly and the Family Stone. Sly was a little out there but wrote some great songs. One of those songs was "Stand." Here are a few lyrics:

> Stand,
> *In the end you'll still be you*
> *One that's done all the things you*
> *set out to do*

> Stand,
> *There's a cross for you to bear*
> *Things to go through if you're goin' anywhere*

> Stand,
> *Don't you know that you are free*
> *Well, at least in your mind if you want to be.*

> Apply yourself. Get all the education you can, but then, by God, do something. Don't just stand there, make it happen.
> ~LEE IACCOCA

There is great power in these words. I am amazed at how many people try to be invisible. They try to hide their light. It is an impossible task because you can be seen in every moment. In my classes, I ask people to stand up to share. I do that because I want people to begin to understand that they must take a stand for their lives. When we dare to show up, to STAND for something, the Universe kicks into high gear and manifestation begins to unfold.

Taking a stand may not be easy but it is essential. The greatest shifts in history have been because someone was willing to stand for a better world. Where are you right now? Are you standing for what you value or believe in? Are you standing for a world that supports us all? If not, why not?

EXERCISE:

- Write down all the ways that you resist standing up for something and for yourself. Journal about what you believe and what you want. Do this without self-judgment.
- Journal what your life would be like if you stood for yourself and your beliefs. Might you be the change you want to see in the world?

affirmation: Today, I am standing for what I believe in. My voice counts.

ANYTHING'S POSSIBLE

There is a song written by Johnny Lang. The lyrics are wonderful and actually very clear about living.

> *Don't …let em tell you you can't be,*
> *Anything you wanna be,*
> *Don't be deceived,*
> *Anything's possible,*
> *If ….you will just believe,*
> *Then you can succeed,*
> *It might not be easy,*
> *But anything's possible.*

One of my clients was diagnosed with an illness and instead of being fearful, she wanted to know the "root" cause. We worked on the core beliefs that were supporting illness in her body. She believed "anything is possible." I had another client with money issues that were devastating. We worked on "the possible" and she later reported in with great news about how things had been resolved.

> If I were to wish for anything, I should not wish for wealth and power, but for the passionate sense of potential— for the eye which, ever young and ardent, sees the possible. Pleasure disappoints; possibility never.
> ~SOREN KIERKEGAARD

We are never promised a life without "shift, challenge or heartache." However, I believe that there is a universal promise that anything is possible. We live in an infinite universe filled with possibilities. That means that we are all capable of living successful, joyous and expansive lives. The question is: through what field of perception are you viewing your life? Are you viewing it from a glass half full or half empty? The point is that you get to choose. I am clear that things are happening now in your life. I am also clear that you get to dictate how you feel and how you choose to respond.

EXERCISE:

- Choose one area in your life that challenges you (e.g., finances, relationships, your work, your creativity).
- Decide that there are possibilities beyond what you see.
- Declare that to be so. Do NOT let anything move you from this declaration. "Anything is possible!" "Everything is possible!" If nothing else, you will invite in peace of mind and that is worth its weight in gold.

affirmation: Today, I call forth the incredible gift of possibility. I am a force to be reckoned with.

POWER

He who controls others may be powerful, but he who has mastered himself is mightier still.

~Lao Tzu

Conscious Choices

From my point of view, to live powerfully is to live from a place that is fully awake. To be fully awake means that we are present in every moment.

On "Connections Radio," the radio show I co-host with Dr. Jordon Paul, we interviewed Dr. Noel Brown, a renowned environmentalist. He shared with us his thoughts on the "precautionary principle," which means to weigh the costs and consequences of every decision. That really caused me to think about the choices we make. Sometimes we make choices to be liked, to feel secure or create safety in a situation or perhaps to gain something. Whatever it is, the decision we make is not about weighing the influence and impact of ourselves and others; this choice moves us out of sync.

> Happiness is a conscious choice, not an automatic response.
> ~MILDRED BARTHEL

Have you reviewed the life choices you are making? Here is a fact: you are living a life based on decisions you made in the past. These past decisions could be unhealthy life choices—such as an unconscious collaboration with people who lack integrity—to keep you from being at a healthy weight or in loving relationships. Whatever they are, you are experiencing the consequence of those choices. This information is not for you to judge but to learn from.

Your happiness depends on how you live your life and the consciousness of your choices.

EXERCISE:

1. Become still, center yourself and journal about areas in your life that you want to expand.
   - Write about past choices that did not support this expansion.
   - Write about past choices that did support this expansion.
2. Take this week to "witness" how you make choices and see if you might want to do things differently.

affirmation: Today, I am aware of all thoughts and choices.

DIVINE DESIGN

For many years in Los Angeles a huge fundraiser was held for Project Angel Food. The event took place at a wonderful and unique space and was a fashion lover's dream come true. At "Divine Design" every top designer donated clothes to raise money. The first week was for VIP's and wealthy invitees, the last week was for shoppers. Each day prices were cut. On the last day, all items were 90% off, with racks and racks of amazing original items, gowns, shoes, bags and more. I was an actress at the time and shopping was a wonderful adventure. I always walked out of there feeling like I was abundant and beautiful from the inside out.

> So I'm true to my unique gifts, and I make space for others. And we all end up winning.
> ~ALAN COHEN

As I thought about this event, it brought to mind that you are a divine design. Each of you is unique and created to be a beautiful work of art. When you recognize this truth, you walk in and out of any space with such a feeling of power and grace that you radiate light and joy. Think about it. What if the most powerful energy in the universe designed you, created you? Wow! That would mean that people would be in search of your gifts to support their lives because of your unique nature. It would mean that people would be in awe of your beauty and could not wait to experience you.

Wouldn't it be wonderful if every person on this planet recognized themselves as a powerfully endowed gift of the universe? Wouldn't it be wonderful if you knew you were an original design created to express joy and happiness?

EXERCISE:

1. Take some time to contemplate your unique design.
   - Your beautiful hair, eyes, and skin
   - Your incredible mind and brilliant ideas
   - Your awesome ability to be with people
   - Your kind and compassionate heart
2. Write these attributes down on beautiful, creative paper and read them every day. Really embody the beauty of you from the inside out.

You were designed for greatness. Step into it each day!

affirmation: Today, I recognize my unique gifts and stand in gratitude.

ANCHORING AUTHENTICITY

I talk about authenticity a lot. I ask people and clients to look at the ways they show up in the world that are real and in alignment with their divine nature. I often receive feedback that some struggle with this. Do you? Is everything fine until something comes up that challenges you and then you lose your voice? It is not uncommon to become afraid to tell the truth or take a stand for what you believe.

> We need to find the courage to say NO to the things and people that are not serving us if we want to rediscover ourselves and live our lives with authenticity.
> ~BARBARA DE ANGELIS

I was once in a situation in which taking a stand could have put my job in jeopardy. I remember feeling constricted; I could not sleep and my mind raced a thousand miles an hour. I conjured up the worst scenarios, which created more anxiety. Then I realized that none of these stories in my mind had happened and that I was miserable by not telling the truth and it could not feel much worse if I did tell the truth. So, I decided to speak. This was one of the scariest moments of my life. Here is the amazing outcome: I did not lose my job, I could finally sleep and the anxiety went away. I discovered that the fear was far worse than the actual event. The true gift is that by being "real" I gained the respect of the people around me and felt better about myself. How are you doing with revealing your authentic self?

EXERCISE: Take some time to be quiet and then contemplate and journal your answers to the following questions.

- Who have I come here to be?
- Am I serving the high vision of my life?

If you are not living up to the answers, surrender the fear and choose differently. The shift in how you feel will be amazing.

affirmation: Today, I recognize that who I am is enough.

HEALING HEARTS

The past couple of years have been hard for people. They have come up against some of their deepest fears and felt challenged in multiple ways. In the individual work that I have been doing with people, we identify areas of the body that feel most constricted. A majority recognize that the heart is the area that feels dense and tight.

> In every community, there is work to be done. In every nation, there are wounds to heal. In every heart, there is the power to do it.
> ~**MARIANNE WILLIAMSON**

I remember being in a workshop and the facilitator was working with me. I was sharing a physical challenge that I was having and he asked me what I think caused it. Without thinking I said, "A broken heart." I was surprised at the answer and then it felt completely right. I had been trying to heal the wounds of my childhood and it was a broken heart.

How are you doing in your life? What is challenging you? Take a moment to stop and close your eyes. Scan your body. If the energy is most constricted in the heart area, it is an indication that a healing is needed there. There are very few people who have not been wounded in the heart by family challenges, betrayals and losses of one kind or another. Whatever it is, it will continue to show in various ways until you heal it.

EXERCISE:

1. Take some time to get still.

99

2. Write down the events and people that have hurt your heart (this may take some time).

3. Pick the top one and write a letter to that person's soul. Tell her (or him) how she hurt you, what lessons you learned and how you will choose differently in the future.

4. Bless the letter and burn it. This symbolizes letting go. Do this as many times as you like with your list. Notice how the heart softens.

affirmation: Today, I invite in the healing of my heart.

Honoring History

Have you thought about the fact that you would not be who you are today if your life did not contain every ounce of living that you have done? Have you thought about the fact that your destiny could not unfold if you did not have the knowledge of your history or "herstory?"

> The more I look around and listen, I realize that I'm not alone. We are all facing choices that define us. No choice however messy is without importance in the overall picture of our lives.
> ~SABRINA WARD HARRISON

I have been working with women in prison for about a year and it has been an extraordinary experience. The four-week workshop I teach is about healing from abuse and trauma. I created this workshop and I am trained, but what creates this trusting connection with the women is that I have lived through similar life challenges as they have. When I speak to them, it is not a concept; I have worked through these issues. My life is a living example of moving beyond experiences that could cause great disconnect.

How about you? When was the last time that you sat down and gave thanks for your life? When did you last give thanks for the good news and the interesting news? When was the last time you literally stopped and stood in gratitude for your amazing life, that you are alive? I encourage you to activate thanksgiving. As I look at my life, gratitude fills my heart. I would not be who I am today without every decision, relationship, job or challenge. I am better because I have lived this life and so are you. The question becomes, have you learned from this life and how will you use the information?

EXERCISE:

1. Write your history and how it has served you, using stream of consciousness writing. This means write what comes out of head and your heart—do not worry about how well it's written.
2. Keep writing and do not edit, or pay attention to punctuation, spelling, grammar, etc.
3. Take some time to give thanks for everything you wrote about.

This is a grand opportunity to love the life you have been given and use it to serve others.

affirmation: Today, I rejoice in this history of my life. It has made me who I am.

PURPOSE

The way you get meaning into your life is to devote yourself to loving others, devote yourself to your community around you, and devote yourself to creating something that gives you purpose and meaning.

~Mitch Albom

Purposeful and
on Purpose

This chapter is about exploring how purposeful you are in your daily life and how on purpose you truly are.

Several years ago, I had the honor of working with author Barry Heerman. He wrote an excellent book entitled *Noble Purpose*. It was written as a journey into finding extraordinary work and life.

> Hide not your talents. They for use were made. What's a sundial in the shade.
> ~**BENJAMIN FRANKLIN**

I want to ask you today, are you feeling on purpose? Are you living an extraordinary life that is filled with purpose, joy and expansion? If you are, hooray! Let us see how we can dive deeper into that experience. If not, let us look at how I can assist you into living from that space. Carlos Castaneda has said that a path is simply a path. It is up to you to be clear about what path you follow and that you do not stay on a path that is unfulfilling, for any reason. This choice MUST be free of fear. I personally have been at many choice points in my life and fear was the only thing that stopped me from following my heart.

Are you in a place of decision making? Do you feel like something bigger is calling you?

EXERCISE: I invite you to look at your life from a place of a powerful witness as you contemplate and journal on the following questions.

- When do I feel the happiest? What am I doing?
- Where am I the most comfortable?
- How am I currently showing up in the world?
- Do I shine my light everywhere that I am?

affirmation: Today, I step boldly into my purpose and experience the birthing of the extraordinary me.

Accountability and Responsibility

One summer my husband and I had our granddaughters with us and it was such a wonderful experience. They were both teens and were experiencing challenges with needing to be responsible. They wanted life's perks but were not always willing to be accountable for their actions or agreements. I remember feeling that way as a teen. Quite frankly, I did not want to work for the things I wanted. That statement makes me smile because I believe this is an area that we all can explore. We don't have to be teenagers. It is easy to be accountable when we feel good about our decisions, but sometimes we realize that we have agreed to something we do not feel like doing. And just like any teen, we get creative in finding ways to ignore the commitment. The only thing that I would point out here is that there is a law of reciprocity: What you put out in the world comes back to you.

> You must take personal responsibility. You cannot change the circumstances, the seasons or the wind, but you can change yourself. That is something you have charge of.
> ~JIM ROHN

Some of us say that we want to be accountable, but then balk at the amount of time and energy it takes to be 100% responsible to our agreements. Every time you break an agreement you are actually breaking a promise and therefore instilling doubt and lack of trust somewhere in your consciousness. Then you begin to draw that same energy to you—the energy of people who do not keep their word or commitments. It is at this point that you begin to feel like a victim, never realizing that you are the one who began this cycle of discontent.

EXERCISE:

1. Take some time to honestly look at your willingness to be responsible and accountable.
2. If you are in integrity, acknowledge yourself.
3. If you are not in integrity, take some time this week to ask yourself how this behavior is taking you off purpose.
4. Now, write down some ways that you are willing to live differently. This will be the beginning of a new level of responsibility. You will be doing it for the expansion of your life.

affirmation: Today, I take full responsibility for my choices. I am a model of integrity.

Trusting the Goodness in Life

I know that the moment you read this title, "Trusting the Goodness in Life," some of you cringed. Why? Because there is a lot going on at this point in time that would not be considered good. Please join me in a dialogue. What if, in everything, goodness existed? What if, at the core of everything, there was the kernel of good?

> That which you create in beauty and goodness and truth lives on for all time to come. Don't spend your life accumulating material objects that will only turn to dust and ashes.
> ~**DENIS WAITLEY**

I once had a client who was contemplating suicide. This person did not see any reason for living and could find nothing in life that was worthwhile. Every week, I prayed that she would continue to show up and work with me. There were moments that she came late, but she came. What we discovered was that she was really uncomfortable with effects that were showing up in her life and the reason they were showing up and causing such distress was because there were unhealed places. Every facet of her current situation was an indicator and reflection of something that had happened in the past. In my counseling with her, we began to look at healing the old energy and how it applied to creating a new life. We began to look for the good memories that were buried under the pain. We began to look in the present and we identified little "rays of light." Those rays blossomed and we opened to recognizing that she was more than capable of creating a new perspective that could support the fulfillment of long-delayed dreams.

I would not wish my childhood on anyone, but it contributed to the work I do today. After the rain, there is clean air. Even after 9-11, people bonded around the world to lift up peace. In some of the most horrific times in history people showed up to nurture and guide people to safety. Wouldn't it be interesting if we, humanity, began to actively look for the good in all things?

EXERCISE: I know it is not easy to find the good in pain, but I promise you that it is possible. Here is a place to start.
- Embrace challenge and stop running from it.
- Stop judging and evaluating defects and look for positive expressions.
- Begin to look at the patterns in life, they are messengers.
- Gratitude is a portal; give thanks for the little things.
- Look for the good news; turn off your television if you need to.
- Acknowledge someone for the gifts they bring.

Here is the most important part: if it exists in one place, it exists as possibility in another. You get to choose how you look at life and respond. The more you see love and beauty, the more it will show up. You can TRUST it.

affirmation: Today, I put my attention on looking for good. Every time I see it I send out a little piece of gratitude.

Igniting Passion and Vision

I am very clear that passion is the foundation for fulfillment of purpose. When the energy of passion is present there is expansion and some level of excitement. Vision is always pulling us. Passion and vision together propel us into a purposeful life.

> I am here for a purpose and that purpose is to grow into a mountain, not to shrink to a grain of sand. Henceforth will I apply ALL my efforts to become the highest mountain of all and I will strain my potential until it cries for mercy.
> ~OG MANDINO

I love Lynne Twist and what she represents in the world. In her book, *The Soul of Money,* Lynne speaks of going into a desert community that was about to die out because of lack of water. She is passionate about indigenous people and supporting them on the planet. Lynne shares that when she arrived in this community, she entered in a circle with the men. The women sat on the outside, but then asked to speak and shared that they had dreams and visions of an underwater lake. Lynne caught the vision and passion of the women to support their communities and they convinced the men to let them dig for water. Not only did they find it, but it opened the field for several nearby villages to connect and build a flourishing community. These women were passionate about caring for their people and it opened, within them, the ability to hear a powerful message.

The passion that lives within you is a signpost to guide you into higher living. There are so many people on this planet "just getting by." That kind of living, I believe, creates disease and overwhelmed people. We are not meant to just exist. We are meant to fly, create, dance and live out loud.

Are you listening to your passion? Are you opening to the high vision of your life? Are you unwavering in your exploration of passionate expression?

EXERCISE:

- Make a commitment to do one thing that you are passionate about, not to gain anything, but just to express it.
- Take time to contemplate your life and ask for the highest vision.
- Write down the thoughts and images that you receive.
- Journal on living your most passionate life and do not hold back. You do not have to know how. You are here to fulfill your purpose!

affirmation: Today, I acknowledge my passion and joyously allow it to flow into my reality.

CHANGE

If there is anything that we wish to change in the child, we should first examine it and see whether it is not something that could better be changed in ourselves.

~Carl Jung

THE PORTALS OF CHANGE

In this chapter we are looking at expanding our consciousness, productivity and expression through the portals of change. If you really think about your life, you will see that at every important juncture, you stepped through a portal and that portal marked a significant change. From elementary school to middle school, from high school to college, single life to married life, embracing parenthood, your first real job,

> If you don't like something, change it. If you can't change it, change your attitude.
> ~MAYA ANGELOU

or moving to another state—no matter what the change, your movement marked a shift. You stepped through a doorway into the unknown.

Sometimes stepping through this portal was easy and grace filled, other times it felt chaotic and challenging. What I would like you to contemplate is the fact that for each change, you chose your experience. Each time you decided whether it was good or bad, enlivening or constricting. The reality of an event cannot be denied. The perception of its effect is up to you.

Some women experience labor for many hours and call it horrible. Other women, who have miscarried many times, look at the same experience as a miraculous unfolding. Someone is hurt and confined to a wheelchair for life. He is angry and bitter. Another takes this experience and becomes a motivational speaker that inspires people to make lemonade out of lemons.

Your attitude is the conductor of the symphony of your life. Don't you think it's time to create the experience you want?

EXERCISE:

Reflect back on an event that occurred in your life.

- How did you choose to respond?
- How are you still responding to that event? What is your perception and how does it affect your choices today?
- I invite you to write about this event and allow it to teach you how you presently look at life and how you respond to changes. Please do not judge, simply witness.

affirmation: Today, I am completely aware that I am the master of my own destiny.

Finances

The period during which this book has been created is a very interesting time on this planet. There is wealth present beyond what most of us can imagine and poverty that is heartbreaking. People are losing jobs and homes; finances are the topic of many intimate circles. Some people are in complete confusion around how to manage retirement funds, shrinking

> Money is not required to buy one necessity of the soul.
> ~HENRY DAVID THOREAU

bank accounts and client bases. Many of the people that I counsel are afraid and panicking.

I had a conversation with a woman whose life was completely changing. She had gone back to school, completed it and was then faced with financial changes. I asked how she was handling it and she said, "I am choosing to simplify, to look at what is really important to me and let the rest go." She chose to be unencumbered! This person stepped through the portal with a new plan for living and managing her finances. She cleared out old things, downsized and moved to be close to family. Creating a new relationship with money supported her. She grasped that money is energy.

I want you to know that a healthy relationship with money had been a life-long challenge for me until I learned to activate faith in an abundant universe, got acquainted with my belief systems around money and decided to put my full attention on shifting my consciousness. It has taken time, but today finances are not an issue. Where are you today?

EXERCISE:

Complete the following statements. If your statements are healthy, make them stronger by creating an affirmation to say every day. If you need work in this area, journal and create an affirmation statement that will reverse your core belief.

- My relationship to money is _____.
- I choose to shift my perception about finances by _____.
- I affirm _____.

affirmation: Today, I relax and embrace money as my friend.

RELATIONSHIPS

There is a song, "Everything Must Change." Of course life changes! I was always looking for love in all the wrong places, thinking someone else would complete me, being devastated when family or friends disappointed me or were out of integrity with their promises. I spent years in the "story" of being abandoned and not enough!

> If civilization is to survive, we must cultivate the science of human relationships—the ability of all peoples, of all kinds, to live together, in the same world at peace.
> ~FRANKLIN D. ROOSEVELT

This is what I want to share with you. The only relationship you really have is to Spirit, God, the Universe, Wholeness, Oneness—however you want to identify the Higher Power. Ultimately, you must get clear about this relationship and how to relate to yourself before you add anyone else to the mix. There is no one outside of you who will take care of you or bring you peace. If you move into a space of deep knowing of your inherent value, you cease to look for anything or anyone outside of you. This is the moment that you can step through the portal of "relational awareness." What I mean is to become aware of how amazing you are and how much you deserve to be loved and to love, to nurture and to be nurtured. You are the one you have been waiting for.

You already have the love you are seeking. Once you are clear about this your vibration goes up and you become a magnet for powerful relationships on every level. I understand that this is not easy, but you must love YOU first!

EXERCISE:

- Write a blessing letter releasing all old, incomplete or unsatisfactory relationships. Include lessons learned, gifts and gratitude.
- Put the letter on alter or sacred place and bless it daily.
- Any time judgment comes in, bless the letter and the people.

affirmation: Today, I actively engage in loving myself.

Conscious Productivity

I am seeing more and more people who are expressing that they feel burned out, exhausted and overwhelmed. They are working harder and achieving less. Whether it is a family pattern or a learned behavior, it does not matter; it is all attached to the belief in struggle. As long as there is struggle consciousness the productivity of your life will suffer. Writers will feel blocked, painters will be unable to paint, par-

> Productivity is being able to do things that you were never able to do before.
> ~**FRANZ KAFKA**

enting will be difficult. The belief in our culture that we must put "pedal to the metal" says that we have to push to achieve. Remember the tale of the tortoise and the hare? The tortoise took a long time and moved on his path. The hare was rushing around, engaged in ego and lost the race.

Rushing around will not make change easier. You will not win the race by being overworked. In the book, *The Corporate Mystic,* there is a story of an executive who committed one day a week to silence in order to renew and refresh. I know most of you cannot or will not do this. However, what if you looked at producing from another perspective? What if the stress was calling you to step through the portal of change into scheduled self-nurturing? What if it is as important as business events? What if you really took the time to rest and believe that this time would support your life?

EXERCISE:

- Really look at how your life is structured.
- If you take time to self-nurture, expand it.
- If you have been too busy for spiritual practice, you are too busy. Schedule at least five minutes a day.
- Plan retreat time just for you, without anyone else accompanying you.

These simple steps will support you in being consciously productive and vital. You deserve it!

affirmation: Today, I am productive from the inside out.

GRATITUDE

Gratitude is the memory of the heart.

~Jean Baptiste Massieu
(translated from the French)

OUR GIFTS AND TALENTS

Every one of us has unique gifts—some seem large and some seem small. They are all powerful gifts regardless of how we label them. Humanity cannot operate without the diversity of each person's uniqueness. Once we learn to acknowledge the power of individual gifts, we will begin to shift the way in which we operate as humanity.

> Gratitude makes sense of our past, brings peace for today, and creates a vision for tomorrow.
> ~MELODY BEATTIE

In this chapter, you are simply going to focus on being grateful for your special gifts. Are you a kind person? Are you a gifted healer? Are you a financial whiz? Whatever it is, I invite you to include in your daily practice joyous appreciation for your gifts.

EXERCISE:

- Every morning spend three to five minutes journaling on gratitude for your gifts. The first day will be easy. Here is the twist: you cannot name the same gift more than once. This means you are being called to dive deep into your consciousness and give thanks for the ways that you show up on this planet and that every day is a gift.

- If there is resistance that pops in, look at this. How often do you negate the gift that you are? Every time that you do, you are creating blocked energy.

- At the end of the writing session, pick one gift that you will affirm throughout the day, e.g., "Today, I give thanks for my gift of compassion." Write it down where you can see it. Say it every chance you get.

You will find that the more you do this, the less time you will have to be dissatisfied or distracted.

affirmation: Today, I am excited to recognize and proclaim the powerful gifts that I possess.

GRATITUDE FOR CHILDREN AND ANIMALS

Being in gratitude anchors a grace-filled life. I love the phrase "Grace is my sufficiency." To me this means that when grace is flowing all our needs are met with ease.

For many of us, our animals are like children, for others our children are at various stages of growth. Whether young or old, our children and animals are our great teachers. They mirror back to us our beauty and our flaws. What if we took time to actually look at the gifts our children and animals provide and give thanks.

Thanksgiving opens the doors. It changes a child's personality. A child is resentful, negative—or thankful. Thankful children want to give, they radiate happiness, they draw people.
~SIR JOHN TEMPLETON

Our task must be to free ourselves...by widening our circle of compassion to embrace all living creatures and the whole of nature and its beauty.
~ALBERT EINSTEIN

My husband and I have two dogs, both are mixes and both have been rescued. They have very different personalities and both are amazing teachers. I used to resist the challenges in their personalities until I had a revelation. They are reflecting back to me spaces that I need to shift. Wow! Big AHA! I began to give thanks for them and my perspective changed. Guess what? I became closer to both of those dogs. I began to see that the places they annoyed me were the places that I needed to heal. The places where they showed love and acceptance were places that lived in me. I then thought: what if I did that for my children, and grandchildren? Something miraculous happened. I started to find new ways to connect and love my family. In return, all of my relationships shifted to a higher level.

EXERCISE:

- Send love and gratitude to your child and/or animal, no matter how they are acting. The soul can hear beyond behavior.
- Be a "love beam" and begin to witness. Do not tell anyone what you are doing. You might be surprised at the shifts that will take place simply because you stand in gratitude for their existence.

affirmation: Today, I send love, honor and respect to all children and animals.

Gratitude for Family and Friends

The people closest to us can push our buttons the most. They seem to know just the right way to pull us into dramatic events and expression. There is someone in my life who I know loves me; however, her childhood was so dysfunctional that connection is erratic. I love to connect, talk and be close. You can imagine how this relationship might tweak me. I used to try to get her attention by calling or texting, hoping she would get how much she is loved. That did not work. I then decided to stop trying to get anything. I decided during my evening meditation to simply give thanks for her in my life. The amazing thing is that I stopped feeling constricted. I recognized that she is doing the best that she can in this moment and does not need my judgment. I have no idea if her behavior will change, but by stopping my neediness I created peace within me and my gratitude for her has to be bringing her love and peace on some level.

> We can only be said to be alive in those moments when our hearts are conscious of our treasures.
> ~THORNTON WILDER

I invite you, in this moment, to really look at anyone who challenges you as an opportunity to give thanks and move into a state of appreciation. This person needs your compassion. By moving into your heart and activating forgiveness, gratitude and peace can fill your soul.

EXERCISE:

- Pick one family member or friend.
- Do not focus on his or her flaws.
- Send gratitude for the ways that this person touches and supports you.
- Simply witness the shift in you.

affirmation: Today, I choose to send love to those who challenge me. I give to them what I want to receive.

GRATITUDE FOR OUR PLANET AND ENVIRONMENT

A study was done that compared the effects of playing music for one group of plants and not playing music for another group. The plants that received the music flourished. Then, the study went further to include praying for a plant and not another. The plants that did not have music or prayer did not do as well. That got me to thinking. What if we applied

> The only work that will ultimately bring any good to any of us is the work of contributing to the healing of the world.
> ~MARIANNE WILLIAMSON

gratitude to our planet and our environment? What if we took some time "beaming" gratitude for the trees, plants, air, water and mountains? What if we actively stopped talking about the dysfunction and instead clearly spoke about the appreciation we have for nature? I am clear we will not turn around global challenges, oil spills or wars that have already happened. However, I truly believe that we are at a universal choice point. We are called to put our attention on the whole, not just our own individual needs.

Recently, I experimented by sharing with people, in detail, why I love where I live. The more I talked about it the better I felt. In fact, it engaged people to talk about what they loved about where they lived and how much they loved caring for their gardens or walking in nature. It was quite cathartic for all of us. Wouldn't it be wonderful if large numbers of people began to talk about how much we love our planet and how grateful we are for all the ways we are supported?

- Your only assignment is to engage other people in conversation about your love for the planet and environment. If they try to pull you into the "what's wrong with the planet" conversation, simply say "I am clear about the challenges, but I want to spend my time focusing on my gratitude for being here and on honoring the gifts of the planet." Who knows, you might experience with another the gift of loving the earth.

affirmation: Today, I celebrate planet Earth. I honor all that it contributes and allow myself to dive into an expanded awareness of our blessings.

SELF-CARE

In dealing with those who are undergoing great suffering, if you feel "burnout" setting in, if you feel demoralized and exhausted, it is best, for the sake of everyone, to withdraw and restore your-self. The point is to have a long-term perspective.

~Dalai Lama

Radical Self-Care

This is a great chapter to visit anytime you need to be reminded and coached to take care of yourself. There are times in our lives when we are unusually busy, and for some people this is a lifestyle. There are family events, holidays, business affairs and with them, sometimes feelings of being alone and even separate. Let us address what I like to call radical self-care: caring for yourself first.

> The more care you put into your life, the more life will care for you, bringing you fun adventures, great friends and real inner security.
> ~DOC CHILDRE

Radical self-care is an interesting and perhaps uncomfortable concept, especially if you have been a caretaker and placed another's needs before your own. It may seem difficult to think about yourself. You may feel there are no other options. You may feel fear that people are going to be upset or annoyed. You may feel there will be some sort of resistance because you have always been the one to handle things. You are probably right. You will be asking people to adapt to a new way of operating with you. They will not understand and will use creative methods to bring you back to the caretaker role. It will be easy to say okay and slip back into the old pattern of doing for others rather than doing for yourself.

Here is the good news. I have discovered over the last several years that the more I take care of myself, the more time and compassion I have available for others. My interaction with other people and the interaction with my career are from a healthy standpoint rather than from need—the need to be validated, the need to be in control, the need to feel important or be loved.

You have the chance to learn how to take care of yourself. You can discover what nurtures you. For me, it's hot baths with candles, walks, meditation and reading great books that feed my soul. It is turning on music and dancing around the house. It makes me feel joyous and alive.

EXERCISE:

No matter what happens, make yourself the priority. Calendar in time to rest and rejuvenate. Remember that NO is a complete sentence. You can decline offers with love and compassion. I believe that you can feel peaceful and fully supported. Take care of yourself, you are worth it!

affirmation: Today, I put myself first and make me the priority. It feels good to be #1.

YOU ARE LOVED

In this section, I would like to support you as you activate a deep remembrance that you are loved. No matter what is happening in your current reality, or what has happened, or even the possibility of what might be hanging over you in the future, this is a time to remember that you are loved beyond measure just because you exist.

> It's so easy to think about love; to talk about love; to wish for love. But it's not always easy to recognize love…even when we hold it in our hands.
>
> ~JAKA

EXERCISE:

Here is a reading from Marianne Williamson's book, *Everyday Grace.* I invite you to breathe in this short reading, entitled, "Starting the Day."

> *It's the beginning of your day*
> *You awake and look around you*
> *Feeling perhaps a joyful expectation*
> *Or perhaps an awful dread*
> *No matter which, REMEMBER THIS*
> *God loves you with an infinite love…*

Print this out and read it every day for a month.

It may seem simple but the truth is, if you can remember that you are loved from a space of infinite love, you will be able to handle any experience. You will understand that you are never alone.

affirmation: Today, I remember that I am loved and important. I am safe, loved and supported.

GIVING AND RECEIVING

M any people find themselves having dual experiences when it comes to family. We are caught between our love of family and dread of the dynamics that often occur. During the holidays, family reunions or vacations, you find yourself in surroundings that are challenging and it is an obligation that we are called to respond to with our presence. I would like you to consider that you can activate faith during this time to pull you through. By activating faith you move into a space of giving and receiving a depth of love that is tangible and profound.

> You give but little when you give of your possessions. It is when you give of yourself that you truly give.
> ~KAHLIL GIBRAN

The following is a passage from a book called *The Source of Miracles* by Kathleen McGowan:

> *Faith is receiving and love is giving*
> *None can receive without faith*
> *And none can give without love*
> *When we believe, we are then capable of receiving*
> *We give so that we may experience love*
> *Whoever gives without love experiences nothing of importance.*

You sharing your love and light is a gift that is valuable in an extraordinary way. You do not have to do anything. The act of you showing up in love is the most powerful thing you can do. This act begins with loving self and then pours out into any arena.

EXERCISE:

Remember that you are the precious gift, always, in any situation. I honor you and give thanks for your presence on this planet.

affirmation: Today, I practice the art of giving and receiving. The result is joy.

CREATING THE LIFE YOU WANT

I t is important that you understand that you have
the power to live a happy and expansive life. Creating the
life you want is the theme for this section. Here is a passage
from *Calling in the One* by Katherine
Woodward Thomas.

> If you do not create your
> destiny, you will have your
> fate inflicted upon you.
> **~WILLIAM IRWIN
> THOMPSON**

You must be able to create a life
that lights you up whether or not
you have a love, a great career, a lot of money, a great
house, a healthy child or a hit song. Part of creating
this magnificent life may include being actively engaged in the pursuit of such blessings. However, to
place the burden of validation of your life upon the
achievement of such things is a terrible encum-
brance. Joy is an unconditional experience that is
not attached to circumstances. It is a choice one
makes to cultivate a consciousness of unconditional
acceptance of what is. In doing so, you free yourself
to feel contentment, happiness, and a deep joy.

EXERCISE:

Whatever is happening in your life, give thanks for what is and vow
to care for your self more deeply than ever before. Journal on this and
then create a non-negotiable agreement that you are the most important person in your life and by caring for you, honoring you, loving

you, you expand the container to love and care for others. Blessings for your work; you are amazing and courageous!

affirmation: Today, I am fearless and dare to step through the portal of my greatness.

About the Author

Cynthia James is a transformational specialist guiding thousands of people to make changes for lasting healing in their lives. As a lecturer, teacher, performing artist and award-winning author of *What Will Set You Free,* she has coached and supported thousands of people into healthy and vibrant living. Cynthia has provided numerous keynotes and facilitated hundreds of workshops and seminars worldwide. She is a featured guide in the movie *Leap!,* the narrator for the CD of the Science of the Mind textbook, a sought-after radio guest, a long-time personal growth blogger for www.GaiamLife.com, and creator of the Cynthia James Support Network. She is also the co-host of Connections Radio for Vividlife.

Cynthia's life was transformed as she rose above her childhood of violence and abuse. Through education and personal healing, she created programs and classes that integrate traditional therapeutic techniques, music, creativity and spiritual processes.

Ms. James graduated from two Masters Degree programs, one in spiritual psychology and one in consciousness studies. She currently serves as an associate minister at Mile Hi Church, Lakewood, Colorado, one of the largest new-thought spiritual centers in the world with a congregation of over 16,000 members and friends. Cynthia lives and thrives in the mountains of Colorado with her husband Carl.

Cynthia James' Music

I Live For Thee
Music to Lift &
Inspire the Heart & Soul

available through CDBaby.com

Transcendence
Vocals & Piano Uplifting Hearts

Piano: Kent Rautenstraus

available through CDBaby.com

Standing in the Light
Music to Celebrate
Our Spiritual Connection

available through CDBaby.com

Remembering Who We Are

(for women only)

available through CDBaby.com

Meditation Series

Spirit of the Inner Child
Finding Your Purpose
Releasing Rage
Transforming Memories

available through CDBaby.com

Cynthia James' Workshops

What Will Set You Free
Weekend Intensive

Set yourself free and come into your power.

Through this integrative experience, each participant is given the opportunity to explore old patterns and expand into new ways of being. This is a transformational workshop that creates a safe space to:

- ❖ Face beliefs that no longer serve you
- ❖ Release old fears
- ❖ Address emotional wounds
- ❖ Claim the full experience that is your life

For information and dates of Cynthia's workshops, write to:
Cynthia@CynthiaJames.net